CAMPFIRE GAMES
& STORIES FOR KIDS

*Interactive camping trip activities for day & night;
outdoor games, would you rather, knock knock jokes,
riddles & nature stories for boys, girls and family fun*

TABLE OF CONTENTS

I. Campfire Games

These games are meant to be played interactively with friends and family while sitting around the campfire. Parents and kids alike can take turns reading from this book and keep the evening interactive by choosing a game to play or joke to read.

The game of names: This is a group activity in which you pick a theme, such as animals, places, or celebrity names. Ask the first player to name something related to the chosen theme, starting with the letter 'A.' From there, players can take turns contributing items to the list, each starting with the last letter of the previous one. For example, if animals are the theme, the game might unfold like this: aardvark, kangaroo, octopus, snake, elephant, and so on. Remember, once an item is named, it can't be used again. Players who can't add a new item during their turn get eliminated until only one victor remains.

20 Questions challenge: Select someone to be 'it.' During each round, this person secretly chooses a person, place, or thing without revealing it to the others. Players then take turns asking 'yes' or 'no' questions about the chosen item, trying to deduce its identity. The catch? There are only 20 questions allowed. If someone correctly guesses the answer, they become the new 'it' for the next round. If not, 'it' is the winner and reveals the identity and a new round begins.

Two truths and a lie: To start, one player shares three statements about themselves – two truths and one lie. For instance, "I have a friend named Annie; On Monday, I went to the school basketball court; and this week, I ate a whole bag of nachos by myself." The other players then try to figure out which statement is false. A correct guess earns a point, and the player with the most points at the end wins.

Fortunately/Unfortunately, storytelling: Kick off the story with a fortunate or positive statement, like "Fortunately, I won the class prize of lunch with the teacher." The next player adds an unfortunate twist, such as, "Unfortunately, the teacher was not present that day, and I had to have lunch with the principal!" The narrative continues with alternating positive and negative contributions. Play goes on until the story reaches a logical conclusion, whether happy or unhappy.

Frog

For this game, you need to gather in a circle by the campfire. It begins when the first person says "ONE FROG," and then the second person adds "2 EYES," the third person puts in "4 LEGS," the fourth person says "IN THE PUDDLE," and the fifth person completes it with a spirited "KER-PLOP." The challenge of the game is to see how many frogs you can get puddled without making any mistakes.

Simon Says

This is played when the first player gives commands and starts with "Simon says." Players are to follow commands that start with this phrase. And if a command is given without "Simon says," and a player follows it, they're out. You can keep the commands simple and mix up the pace to keep players engaged. Make your own list or use the list at the end of the book.

Scavenger Hunt

This is simple and allows everyone to create a list of items or clues for participants to find around the campfire. The first team or individual to find everything wins. Customize the hunt based on the campfire's location and age group. See pages near the end of the book.

Flashlight Tag

This is a twist, on tag played in the dark. The "it" player uses a flashlight to tag others. Once tagged, a player also becomes "it." For safety, you can set boundaries to make sure players are cautious in the dark.

Nature Bingo

In this bingo game, you can play with pinecones, colorful leaves, or animal tracks. Participants can then mark off items once they find them. Also, you can adjust difficulty based on the age group and offer prizes for completing the bingo card. Fill in the blank templates at the end of the book and make your own bingo game.

A-Z Story

The first player starts the first sentence of the story with the letter "A". For example: "Albert went to the store one day." The next player adds a sentence with the letter "B", and so on until you finish the alphabet. You can also start with "Z" and work backwards.

10 in 10
Player 1 picks a category, for example animals. The other players come up with 10 examples as fast as they can, the player that created the category can judge who finishes first and who gave the best examples.

Who am I?
Player 1 thinks of a character from a movie or book to keep in mind while the other players ask questions to discover "Who am I?"

Secret Message
Sit in a circle around the campfire, Player 1 whispers a short message in Player 2's ear. Player 2 whispers what they heard to Player 3, and so on until the last Player says it out loud. Usually, answers are quite funny, Player 1 then corrects them.

I Spy
Players take turns saying "I Spy with my little eye, something that is….", other players guess. The winner gets a point.

Tongue twisters

Have players repeat each tongue twister as many times as they can in one minute. The winner is the one with the highest number of clear repetitions. Some examples are:

- Rusty the rooster roasts red raspberries.
- Freddy fox fried fresh fiddlesticks.
- How much wood could a woodchuck chuck, if a woodchuck could chuck wood?

Guess the number

Player 1 thinks of a number in their mind between 0 and 50. The other players take turns asking questions to discover the number. For example: "Is it odd?", "Is it in the 40's?"

Shopping List

Players take turns adding an item to an imaginary shopping list. Before you add your item you must remember and recite all the previous items. If they can't finish the list the next player tries. Players get another chance when their turns come around and the goal is to make the list as long as possible. For example: Player 1: "Cheese", Player 2: "Cheese, Bread."

Never Ever have I Ever

Sitting around the campfire, each person holds out there hands so everyone can see there fingers. The first player says "Never Ever have I Ever _____" been to Europe, skydived, etc. It works best if they pick something they think no one has done. If a player has done it they put one finger down (fold it under their hand). The last person with fingers up is the winner.

II. WOULD YOU
RATHER QUESTIONS

Read the questions out loud and let everyone answer them or read them by yourself. Circle the words you choose or write people's names next to their choice.

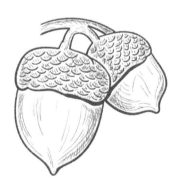

1. Would you rather:

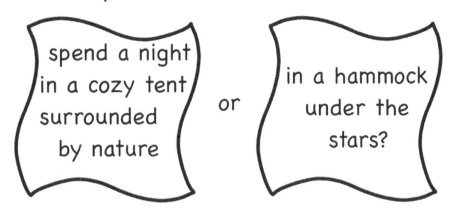

spend a night in a cozy tent surrounded by nature

or

in a hammock under the stars?

2. Would you rather:

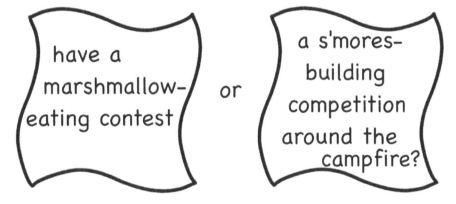

have a marshmallow-eating contest

or

a s'mores-building competition around the campfire?

3. Would you rather:

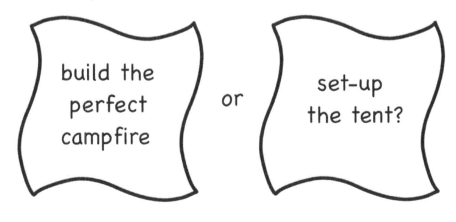

build the perfect campfire

or

set-up the tent?

4. Would you rather:

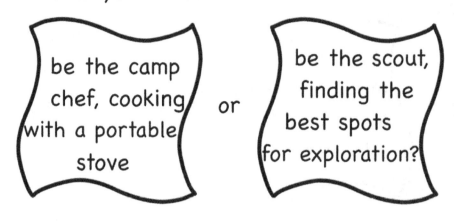

be the camp chef, cooking with a portable stove

or

be the scout, finding the best spots for exploration?

5. Would you rather:

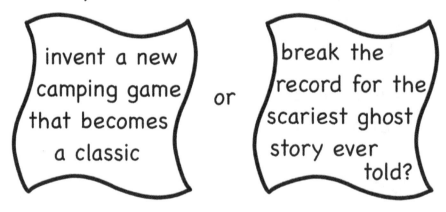

invent a new camping game that becomes a classic

or

break the record for the scariest ghost story ever told?

6. Would you rather:

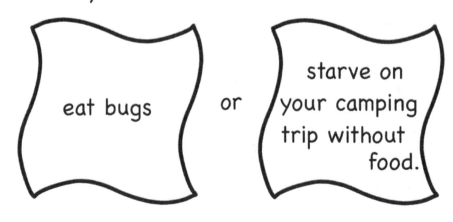

eat bugs

or

starve on your camping trip without food.

7. Would you rather:

have a rainstorm   or   a snowstorm while you are camping?

8. Would you rather:

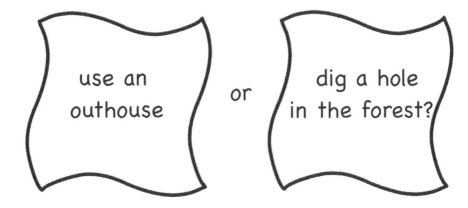

use an outhouse   or   dig a hole in the forest?

9. Would you rather:

hike   or   drive to your campsite?

10. Would you rather:

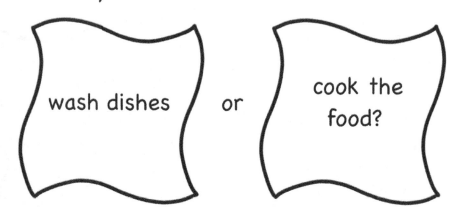

wash dishes or cook the food?

11. Would you rather:

find a snake or a mouse in your tent?

12. Would you rather:

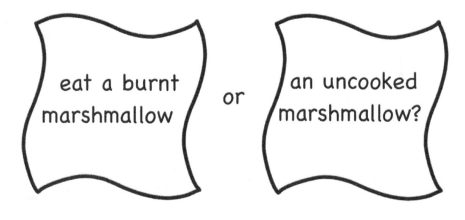

eat a burnt marshmallow or an uncooked marshmallow?

13. Would you rather:

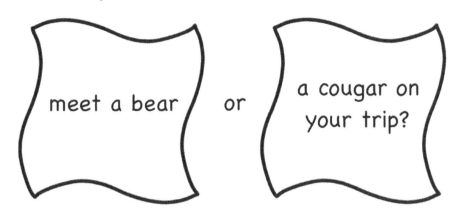

meet a bear   or   a cougar on your trip?

14. Would you rather:

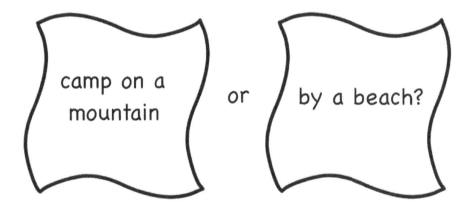

camp on a mountain   or   by a beach?

15. Would you rather:

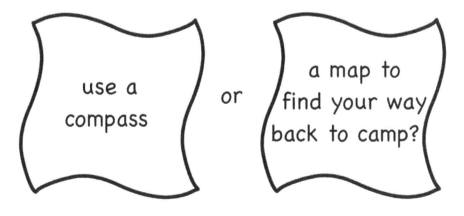

use a compass   or   a map to find your way back to camp?

16. Would you rather:

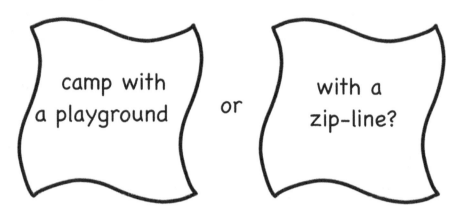

camp with a playground   or   with a zip-line?

17. Would you rather:

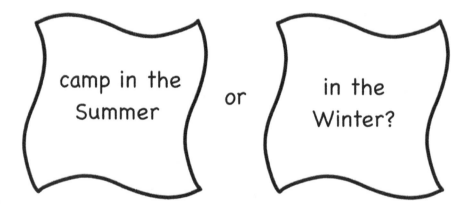

camp in the Summer   or   in the Winter?

18. Would you rather:

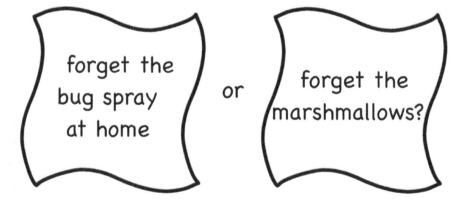

forget the bug spray at home   or   forget the marshmallows?

19. Would you rather:

not have a bath for a week **or** jump in a cold lake to clean-up?

20. Would you rather:

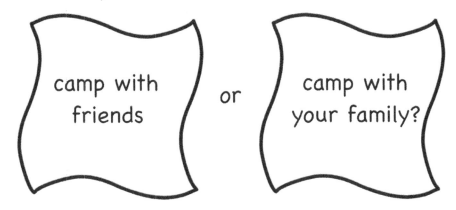

camp with friends **or** camp with your family?

21. Would you rather:

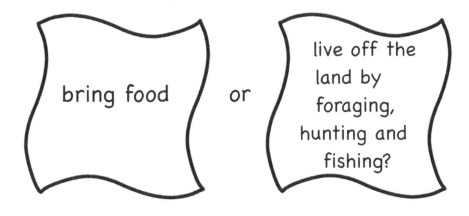

bring food **or** live off the land by foraging, hunting and fishing?

22. Would you rather:

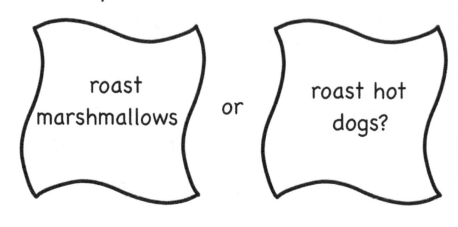

roast marshmallows **or** roast hot dogs?

23. Would you rather:

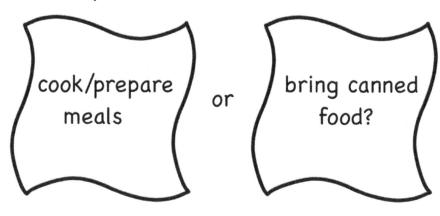

cook/prepare meals **or** bring canned food?

24. Would you rather:

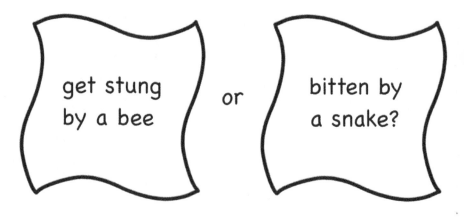

get stung by a bee **or** bitten by a snake?

25. Would you rather:

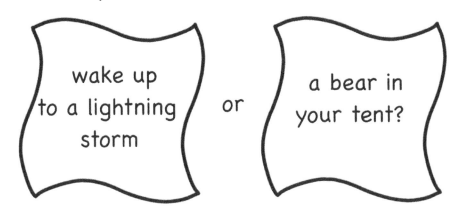

wake up to a lightning storm   or   a bear in your tent?

26. Would you rather:

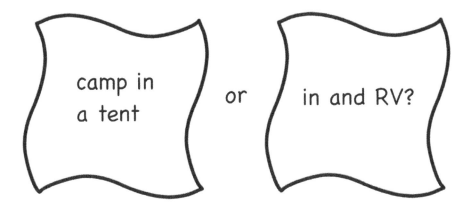

camp in a tent   or   in and RV?

27. Would you rather:

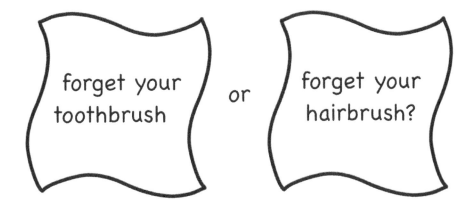

forget your toothbrush   or   forget your hairbrush?

28. Would you rather:

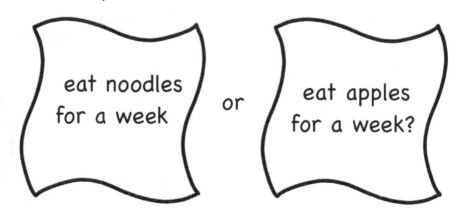

eat noodles for a week or eat apples for a week?

29. Would you rather:

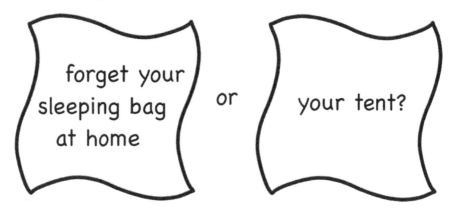

forget your sleeping bag at home or your tent?

30. Would you rather:

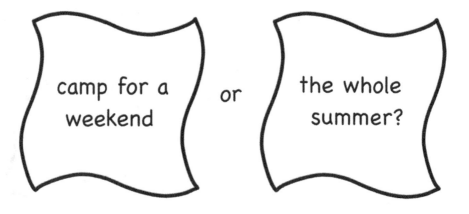

camp for a weekend or the whole summer?

III. Jokes and Riddles

When you want to lighten up the atmosphere try reading out these jokes and riddles.

Knock knock jokes

Knock, knock
> Who's there?
> Hatch.
> Hatch who?
> Hatch you on the trail, let's go exploring!

Knock, knock
> Who's there?
> Justin.
> Justin who?
> Justin time for the marshmallow roast!

Knock, knock
> Who's there?
> Lettuce.
> Lettuce who?
> Lettuce in, it's getting dark out here!

Knock, knock
> Who's there?
> Cow says.
> Cow says who?
> No silly, Cow says mooo!

Knock, knock
> Who's there?
> Atch.
> Atch who?

Bless you! Must be the campfire smoke.

Knock, knock

Who's there?

Wanda.

Wanda who?

Wanda s'more before bedtime?

Knock, knock

Who's there?

Alpaca.

Alpaca who?

Alpaca the bug spray, we don't want any mosquito bites!

Knock, knock

Who's there?

Fire.

Fire who?

Fire up the grill, it's dinner time!

Knock, knock

Who's there?

Honeydew.

Honeydew who?

Honeydew you know how to set up a tent?

Regular jokes

1. Why don't oysters go near the campfire?
   Well silly, they're afraid of getting shell-shocked.

2. What do you call a bear with no teeth at the campground?
   A gummy bear!

3. What do you call cheese that isn't yours at the campfire?
   Nacho cheese!

4. Why did the mosquito say at the campfire party?
   It was a bite to remember.

5. What did one sleeping bag say to the other at the campfire area?
   I'll cover for you.

6. Why did the camper bring a ladder to the campfire?
   To roast the marshmallows on a higher flame.

7. What's a camper's favorite type of humor?
   In-tents!

8. Why don't fish go camping?
   They are always in schools!

9. What do you call a bear with no shoes?
   Bear-foot!

10. What did the tent say to the sleeping bag?
    Zip it!

11. Why don't tents ever get into arguments?
Because they know how to keep things pitched perfectly!

12. How do you organize a campfire under the stars?
You planet!

13. What did one mosquito say to another at the campfire?
Buzz off, I'm trying to eat here!

14. Why did the bear bring a ladder to the campfire?
Because it wanted to reach the high-bear-nation level!

15. What's a vampire's favorite type of camping?
Steakouts in the woods!

16. Why did the squirrel bring a suitcase to the campfire?
It wanted to pack up for a nutty vacation!

17. How do you start a bear race from the campfire?
Ready, teddy, go!

18. What did one camping tent say to the other?
"You're un-be-weave-able!"

19. Why did the camping chair go to therapy?
It had too many issues with being foldable!

20. What did the marshmallow say to the chocolate at the campfire?

"You make life s'more fun!"

21. Why did the tree go to the campground?

It wanted to get to the root of the outdoor experience!

22. Why did the camping stove break up with the campfire?

It couldn't handle the heat!

23. How do you plan a camping trip with mushrooms?

You spore-ganize it!

24. Why do campers always carry a pencil?

In case they want to draw on their resources!

25. Can a frog jump higher than a tent?

Of course, a tent can't jump.

Riddles

Riddle 1

In the forest's heart, with the tall standing trees,
You can call me a portable home, not very big, not very small.
I am made with fabric walls and a roof of nylon
I provide shelter at dawn; what am I?

A tent

Riddle 2

Days turn into nights, and the skies get clear,
You can only find me looking up,
I twinkle and sparkle, a celestial art,
I play a role in nature's chart. What am I?

Stars

Riddle 3

I'm a gathering place in the evening hours of your campsite
Flames dance on my logs, and I make them blush.
I can make your marshmallows skewered and toasted,
I am where memories are made.
What am I?

Campfire

Riddle 4

I have no COVID, but I have a mask on my eyes and fur on my back,

I walk, run and climb through the woods.

Not a bear, but similarly handsome,

Who am I?

Raccoon

Riddle 5

I wind through the bush in a narrow winding lane,

I carry the marked footsteps of hikers, adventurers

Although I am a little small for a car, but for those on a quest,

I can lead you on an enjoyable journey.

What am I?

Trail

Riddle 6

I'm tied with precision between two strong arms (trees)

Call me a swinging cocoon, a relaxation decision.

But I am not a bed in a room

What am I, swaying gently in the forest?

Hammock

Riddle 7

I'm the force that ignites, but I do not need a match or a lighter,

Yet, without me, a campfire's glow grows quieter.

When you rub sticks together, I can create a spark in the night,
What am I?

Friction

Riddle 8
Made of metal, I am sturdy and stout,
Sure, I can provide a flame in the wild, there's no doubt.
I am not a hearth at home, but surely all camper's best friend,
On me you cook meals under the starlight,
What am I?

A camp stove

Riddle 9
I'm a canvas of stories, you look at me and narrate them,
A masterpiece changing colors for all to enjoy.
Sometimes I weep, with raindrops that fall,
I span over, covering all.
What am I?

Sky

Riddle 10
I'm a guardian on your head for those raindrops descending,
With a cover embracing you, my protection won't end.
I am not very sturdy, nor have I walls, but a shelter free, standing tall,
What am I?

An umbrella

IV. Scouting and Nature Games

These games and activities can be played with family and friends. Add variations to mix it up.

Treasure hunts

A treasure hunt excites everyone sitting in an outdoor gathering. Treasure hunts require some preparation ahead of time. And don't forget to bring a pencil on your trip. Let's have a look at the step for planning a treasure hunt. There are blank maps near the end of the book.

- **You can craft a story:** You can create a fantasy story centered around the treasure to increase the excitement of the players. For example, consider having themes like pirates, explorers, or ancient artifacts.
- **Create clues creatively:** Make a sequence and put some challenging clues in it. But do not keep the difficulty level too high. So, in that way, the participants get to use their brains and eventually get closer to the treasure.
- **Select locations:** Considering a location, for example, near natural landmarks and manmade structures, will help you fit clues more easily.
- **Make teams:** Participants can work in teams. And the first team to find all the clues and get to the treasure wins.

Here are some of the treasure hunt-themed styles of games to try out on your camping trip:

Puzzle pieces: The puzzle piece game can be played near the campfire. Hide the pieces of the puzzle nearby. This challenge can be to create a bigger picture by finding the pieces of the puzzle that are scattered around. Teamwork can shine in this one. Each team can have a person solving and rearranging the pieces, one who finds the pieces. You can use the blank pages at the end of this book to create your puzzle.

Compass challenge: This is a game in which each child needs a compass and a set of coordinates and will help you improve your navigation skills. The game is that each player has to reach the targeted points marked on the map. On each coordinate, they will have some challenges and clues that will take them closer to the final destination. This type of treasure hunt will help the players know much more about direction, coordination, and reading a map.

Codebreaker: This fun game that can be played around the campfire. The game involves having a coded message that needs to be deciphered and, in return, that will reveal the location of the treasure. Participants can be called amateur cryptographers in this game (as they solve puzzles to crack locations). This game will promote critical thinking as well as problem-solving skills.

Nighttime glow hunt: Since we are talking about games around the campfire, how can this be missed? This one carries an extra thrill of finding the treasure at night. What highlights the game is the use of glow sticks that can be used to mark the trail and for the treasures. Pparticipants need their own flashlights. It's a suspenseful yet exciting game to play under the stars that create a memorable hunting experience.

Time travel hunt: Well, it's a game in which you can incorporate the theme of time travel. How? Create clues for each step representing a different era. And the participants must follow each era one by one to reach the destination. At last, it will be like coming out of a "Time capsule." Isn't this one engaging and imaginative?

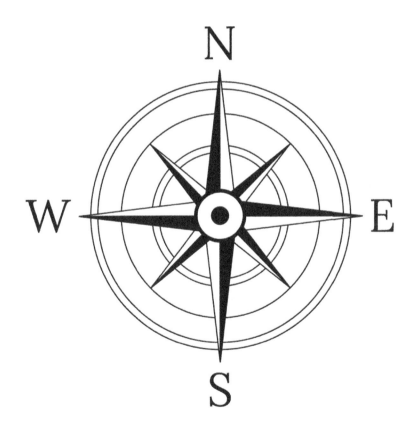

More Games and Activities

Outdoor movie night: You can set up a screen and projector to watch movies under the stars near the campfire. You can also buy projectors that use your cell phone to project the image onto a sheet, you will need to plan this activity ahead of your trip. Have some marshmallows ready and some popcorn. Choose holiday-themed or camp-themed movies and test your audio-visual set-up before your trip.

Hot Seat: For this game, you need to position one person's chair facing the group, and this person's chair is now the 'HOT SEAT.' Then, write a funny word on a piece of paper and show it to everyone sitting on the other side of the hot seat player. The task here is to make the person sitting in the hot seat guess that word by offering him hints and clues. If the person answers correctly, then they win. If not, then a lighthearted penalty can be given to that person, like singing a song, making some dance moves, or imitating a funny performance.

Laser Tag: This can be played by using outdoor-friendly laser tag sets for a high-tech version of the tag. It's a game in which players aim to "tag" opponents with lasers. But make sure the area is safe and has some clear boundaries.

Scouting Games

Each activity can be played with teams if you have enough people, or complete each challenge collaboratively by working together.

Knot tying relay: This is an engaging challenge. Participants are trained with techniques through many sessions before the final competition. The relay race is where two teams compete, and the winner is the one who ties the knot first and fastest. Both precision and speed are checked. Also, the instructions that are to be followed by the teams must be given beforehand.

Fire building competition: This is not just a game but something that will instill and make you learn how to build a fire, an important outdoor survival skill. Arrange a friendly competition to see which team can build fire sustainably first. The challenge involves collecting the materials needed to start the fire, like the right tinder and kindling. The judges will be choosing the winner based on  factors like speed, sustainability, and how long the fire lasts.

Orienteering: This activity can turn learning navigation into an adventurous game for anyone. A course is set and marked with some checkpoints on a map, and a compass is used to navigate through the campsite, finding each checkpoint in sequence. This game allows you to learn to interpret maps, follow compass directions, and make decisions on the best route to reach each checkpoint. Orienteering is an exciting blend of mental and physical challenges during camping.

First aid and nursing: When one participates in activities away from home such as camping, the chances of getting hurt are higher. In the game, players can simulate first aid scenarios where they assess emergencies and injuries. For example, each team is presented with different scenarios to test their knowledge and application of first aid principles. This game reinforces the importance of being prepared for unforeseen situations outdoors.

Campfire skits: Campfire skits are a fun and humor-filled challenge. For this game, kids can be divided into small groups, and the challenge is to craft short skits or performances. These performances can range from comic sketches to educational nature pieces. The real magic of these skits is the gathering around the campfire, which sets a warm and collaborative atmosphere.

Survival bracelet workshop: The survival bracelet workshop gives you a hands-on experience activity. They learn the art of making survival bracelets using paracord. Sure, they need to be guided by skilled instructors to know about the various knots and weaving techniques. Paracord bracelets are a functional accessory during camping.

Campfire cooking contest: The campfire cooking contest gives you a chance to show off your chef skills. You can work together or in teams to make a delicious meal. For example, one person could handle chopping, another could supervise, and a third person could take care of cleaning. This contest can build up love for outdoor cooking and explore the cooking talents of young campers.

Water purification challenge: Knowing about water purification is a hands-on and educational experience. In this challenge, you prepare to face challenges like dealing with contaminated water. You must purify it using tools like filtration devices, purification tablets, or other available methods. The one thing this challenge requires is to work in collaboration and make sure water becomes safe for consumption. This activity not only imparts practical knowledge but also teaches the significance of clean water in outdoor adventures, promoting responsible and safe camping practices.

Survival Skills Challenge: This can be played by setting up stations for basic survival skills. For example, knot tying, fire starting, and shelter building. Teams rotate through the challenges. This is one game that can teach you valuable skills while being competitive and fun.

Nature Games and Activities

Bird watching: For this game, all the participants need guides and binoculars. The game is to identify as many bird species as possible and note their names. To make it more of a team-building game, divide participants into teams.

Leaf and tree identification: For this activity, a scavenger hunt type game can be arranged in which the players must choose different types of leaves and trees. This game helps in learning about local vegetation while also having fun.

Nature art workshop: Another game that involves nature and natural elements is collecting and arranging natural materials in a workshop. To start the game, make two teams and provide each team with a list of items they have to collect. For example, let one team collect rocks (different types) and another one collect leaves. Later, they can make some artwork using what they have collected. Bonus if you remembered to bring glue on your trip.

Camouflage hide and seek: Hide and seek is basic, but this one is an upgraded version. In this game, participants have to wear earth-toned camouflage clothes to blend into nature easily. And then, the seeker has to find the camouflaged players. The best part is that this game can be played nearby your campsite.

Nature trivia: This is more of an educational game rather than just fun. For this, select some players and ask them to prepare questions from the camping and campfire process. You can play this game on the last day of the trip. Include as many questions as possible from the events that happened during the trip.

Nature photography contest: Today's generation is fast, and everyone nowadays owns a phone. This is one thing that will make your camping fun. How? You can get beautiful shots of nature. To encourage more creativity, you can choose specific themes and categories.

DIY craft station: You can set up a crafting area with materials for nature-inspired crafts like leaf rubbings, rock painting, or friendship bracelets. This is something that will encourage creativity and allow campers to take their crafts home as souvenirs.

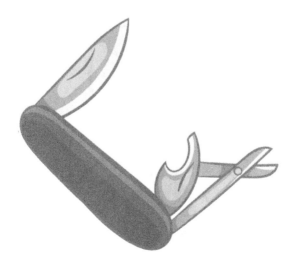

v. Campfire Stories

Stories can be read silently or around the fire. Write a story independently or with your group. Each person can take turns adding to the story.

- Mystic Mountain
- Joe and his Forest Friends
- Whispering Pines
- The Unexpected Storm
- Write your own Story

Mystic Mountain

I looked out of the car window as the buildings disappeared and a continuous forest of trees surrounded the car as we continued the drive up the mountain. I was so excited to begin six weeks of summer camp at Mystic Mountain. I had just turned eleven years old, and I could not contain my excitement for my summer adventures. I had heard stories from my father about this mountain, about summers years ago that he spent here. I am not sure who was more excited for me to go, me, or him!

As my Dad drove the car up the long dirt road to the entrance of the camp, there was a clearing that revealed a sight that seemed to be straight out of a book! There were tall pine trees, a crystal clear lake and I could smell the campfire that was just getting started. This was it. The place that promised mystery and exciting quests. I stood there for a few minutes, taking it all in. We headed to the registration table and I quickly hugged my parents bye. I set my duffle bag down on the top bunk in the cabin and headed outside to explore.

I couldn't help but be in awe of the beauty, and excited for the unknown. I heard the sounds of chirping birds and the wind blowing the leaves. Yup, I had just transformed into the main character in a storybook, and I was about to begin an epic quest.

I met up with a group of fellow campers, they were getting ready for the evening campfire. Nervously, I approached the group and introduced myself. The faces, while unfamiliar now, would soon become three of my best friends that summer. As it turned out, their fathers had also attended this summer camp. We spent the days swimming and hiking, among some of the other camp activities. The nights, however, were spent around the fire, sharing stories and laughter as the stars shone on the lake. I was unaware at the time of the role these new friends would play in unraveling the mystery that was in store.

It was a warm afternoon, and we were digging for arrowheads near the lake when my shovel hit something hard about 10 inches underground. Excited to unearth something amazing, like a fossil, I got down on the ground and began digging with my hands. It was a metal box, about the size of a cereal box. I cleared away the dirt to figure out how it opened. As I shook the box, the lid moved and I began pulling the top aside. It was not an easy thing to do, it was rusted and didn't want to budge.

Finally, I was able to slide the lid to the right to reveal the contents. What I saw was nothing short of disappointing. It was just a few trinkets, a compass, an old photo of three boys that was taken next to the lake, there was something oddly familiar about their faces - but they were obviously too old for us to know them. Also in the box was an old weathered piece of paper, its edges frayed, and its surface yellowed with age.

Carefully, I unfolded the paper, it looked to be a hand-drawn map of the campgrounds, with a big red "X" marked in a spot deep in the woods, not far off the trail. There were also a series of initials in the lower left corner, "J.K." "P.D." and "J.P". Were these the initials of the mysterious authors? Perhaps, but we couldn't know for sure.

Also written were the words:

Look for a formation that is not naturally there,
The rocks are stacked, with magical flair.
Go along the trail, embrace the view,
Under the rocks, the prize waits for you.
Crack the riddle, be sharp and clever,
Discover the treasure, or it will be hidden forever.

Now this was exciting! The map had awakened an interest in hidden treasure, curiosity and excitement that sent a wave of electricity through my body. I called my buddies over and we spread the map out by the lakeside. Everyone gathered around intrigued by what lay before them. The faded ink showed trails, landmarks and the possibility of a journey that we were all too anxious to begin. I folded the map up, put it back in the box and took it to my cabin.

Later that evening, word had begun to spread around the camp about a long-lost treasure that was buried there on the grounds. Campers added exaggerated details and the story had all the makings of a magical adventure. Everyone's imagination was running wild! The stage was set for an unforgettable quest for sure.

Back in the cabin, three of my friends and I looked at the map by flashlight. We tried to decipher the clues. We made the decision that the next night, we would start to uncover the secrets that whoever buried this map wanted to hide. This was just the beginning and to say we were anxious to begin was quite an understatement.

Each night we gathered together, looked at the riddle, and used the compass to navigate our way through the trails and woods. We took note during the day of rocks and things along the path that we could return to at night. We worked together as a team, as three friends on a shared mission. Nightly exploration became our routine. We would head out after dinner, but be back before it was time for the campfire. Sometimes we got lost for a bit, but we always found our way back to the fire.

As the nights went on, we went deeper into the veil of darkness, with the thrill of the unknown fueling us to solve this mystery. We laughed as wildlife, shadows and clumsiness kept us on our toes. I began to notice familiar landmarks and was reminded of my father's stories about his time here at Mystic Mountain. Like the old rope swing he said they used to jump off into the lake, and the fishing pier he said he caught the biggest bass fish he had ever seen. It was almost like this map was a time machine, linking his childhood with mine.

We discovered small artifacts along the way, clues left behind decades ago by the map's authors. It was all coming together like a puzzle, but the location of the treasure was still unknown. Finally one night we found a rock formation that looked like it didn't belong there. Excitement filled the air, had we finally found the elusive treasure? We stood there, in shock and anxious to reveal the secrets of Mystic Mountain.

We quickly began removing the rocks, one by one, they got bigger as we got down closer to the ground. We had to lift them together as they were heavy! We moved a final rock and began to dig. About 6 inches into the dirt, we uncovered another metal box. This one was a bit bigger than the box we had found by the lake earlier that summer.

We pulled the box out of the protection of the rocks and eagerly looked at it. The box wasn't heavy, but there was definitely something in it. The years of hot humid summers had rusted the top, sealing the contents inside for who knows how long. It took quite some time, and all three of us pulled the lid off. It broke free and we went tumbling down to the ground from the release.

We saw a blue Cubs hat, a slingshot, and a pocket knife. The knife was small with a 2″ blade and a wooden handle that had the initials "J.P." engraved. There was also another old piece of paper, equally as worn and aged as the map. Gently I unfolded the paper, revealing a handwritten message.

"Wow, you found it! You are a real-life treasure hunter - or maybe you are a pirate and expecting a chest full of gold, sorry to disappoint you if that's the case.

As you can see, this chest isn't full of shiny gold coins - but it does contain our most prized possessions and memories of the best summer ever!

Hope you enjoyed the adventure and made your own memories solving our mystery!

Sincerely,

JK, PD and JP

There was one more item in the box, a photo of three boys. The same three boys from the first photo, but this time, they were posed in front of the rocks. It looked like the photo was taken right where we were. One of them was wearing the Cubs hat, one had a slingshot in his pocket and the other was cutting a fishing line with his pocket knife.

So these boys were the authors of the treasure map. Now the random items made sense. I handed the photo to one of my friends and as he looked at it, I noticed some writing on the back.

John Kent, Paul Dunn and Jack Parson (aka J.K., P.D. and J.P.)

I snatched the photo back and read the names again, this could not be happening. How had I not put these things together? J.P. Those are my dad's initials and now, written in front of me, was his name. Jack Parson. I stared at the photo, that's why it looked familiar. This time I saw my own eyes staring back at me. This was a photo of my father. This pocket knife was his. I excitedly told my friends about the discovery and we all agreed, that I should keep the knife. In its place, I dropped an arrowhead I had found the first time we went digging that summer.

We flipped the old piece of paper over and signed our names - and I added a quick note about replacing the knife with my prized arrowhead and how the treasure hunt was created by my father. We closed the box up, with the note and photo and reassembled the rock formation.

When we returned to the cabin, we signed the back of the map and placed it in its old box. We would bury the box in the same place we found it, the next day, in hopes that some other group of friends would have an unforgettable quest in the future, perhaps even my own son one day!

Since word of the treasure map had spread around the camp, we excitedly ran back to the fire to tell everyone about the discovery. To be honest, they were a little disappointed that it wasn't a box of gold, but I understood the importance of the shared experience and memories. This adventure proved that magic can be found in the simplest of things in life, connection to those who had come before us.

While the rest of the summer was fun, nothing could top this grand adventure. As summer camp ended, I was grateful for the fun, friends and curiosity that led us to value tradition and connection. I said goodbyes to my friends, not sure if I would ever see them again.

I got into the passenger seat of the car and as my dad drove down the mountain, I looked back, hoping to return here one day. My dad asked about my time at camp. As I told stories about hiking and swimming, and digging for arrowheads, I pulled the beloved pocket knife out of my backpack.

I handed the knife to my dad who looked at it, it took him a moment to realize what it was, but once he did, a smile crept across his face. I could tell he was thinking about his friends and that adventurous summer they decided to bury a treasure on Mystic Mountain.

Joe and his Forest Friends

"I know, Joe, you have a heart for wildlife, but we can't let them ruin our garden! Right?"

Natalie, his mom, was wrapping the woodpecker hole with burlap and talking with her son. Joe stood there thinking of the poor woodpecker whose home was being sealed by his mother while the bird was away.

He remembered the times when his mother used to stuff the hole with a cloth; he could take it out to give Woodie the woodpecker back his nest.

"Do you understand?" Natalie burst the bubble of his thoughts. He looked at her and nodded in agreement. Joe stood there with flooded eyes, looking at the sealed abode of his now homeless birdy bud.

Natalie was headed inside of the house when she turned, "Have you packed for your forest camping trip?" he didn't bother to turn around and stood with his back to his mother.

Natalie stood there waiting for his response.

"Yes," he swallowed back his tears.

"Try to avoid any silly antics at the camp. Just do whatever Mr. Landers says." She left while Joe stood there grieving for Woodie's home.

The next day, Joe was standing in his forest camp, awestruck at the towering trees and the dappled sunlight, which turned everything into a golden glow with an earthy fragrance. Their forest camp was nestled close to the lush wilderness. It seemed like a gateway to the world of jaw-dropping mysteries waiting to be discovered.

He was in a "pinch-me" moment and excitement bubbled within his body. His brain started visualizing days filled with thrilling adventures and discoveries inside the heart of nature which stretched out right before him.

He could feel the symphony of birds chirping as if they were humming a rhythm. He could feel the rustling leaves sharing ancient stories with him. Poor Joe didn't realize he was living in a dreamland until Mr. Landers announced:

"Ok, kids, listen up! I know you all are eager to explore the forest, but unfortunately, we can't! We won't venture too far inside the forest. We have been informed by the local community about the potential wildlife dangers. A bear has been spotted nearby!"

A wave of fear crept among the students.

"Shushhh! Do not worry; we are safe here, and we have taken all the precautions." He continued,

"As far as your entertainment is concerned, we will have sessions on interesting facts about wildlife and we'll also play different games."

The announcement deflated Joe's excitement like a balloon, and a wave of disappointment flashed across his face. On his way to camp, he imagined himself going through the dense foliage, interacting with the untamed environment, and discovering the other side of nature. All the kids were happy they were safe, but Joe wanted this trip to be memorable. He knew where there is a will, there is a way! His contemplative face turned bright. He grinned from ear to ear.

"Come on, Becca, this is a once-in-a-lifetime experience; we can't waste our day listening to Mr. Landers' boring outdoor lectures; we should explore the forest life," Joe whispered to his friend in rather a pleading tone.

The minutes passed by while both the kids bickered about Joe's wild idea to explore the forest. Becca's eyes were starry, but her prudent mind kept telling her the worst scenarios, including getting in trouble for disobeying. In the end, the starry eyes won, and the worst scenarios settled down at the back of her subconscious. After all, she wanted to be like her mother, a wildlife enthusiast who lived to study wildlife and their habitat.

Both the kids quietly snuck out of their tent and exited the camp, dodging the eyes of Mr. Landers and the other students. They strolled through the narrow trail into the forest, getting awe-struck by its astonishing greenery and the aroma of sweet flowers nearby. Joe could see nature in its glory when the sunlight filtered through the leaves like a golden embrace, filling the air with the warmth of life. The filigree of the leaves and the canopied trees made them wonder if it was real or if they were in a fairytale.

It was then when they heard a voice growling, "Help!"

They stood facing each other, locking eyes in mutual bewilderment.

"Joe?" Becca quivered.

"Run!" Joe yelled, and both started running.

After they had run a short distance, reality hit Becca, and she stopped. "What?" asked Joe, who had stopped after realizing Becca wasn't running anymore.

Bent down on her knees, Becca gasped heavily and said, "We should help!"

It took a few moments for Joe's guilt to gush in. For sure, they were wrong to leave a needy person alone. When they went back, they found a huge brown bear lying on the ground. His foot was caught between two rocks and he couldn't move.

"Is it dead, Joe?" asked Becca in a somber tone.

"No, look, he is breathing! He is alive. We just need to help him with…"

"Ohh! Poor Rex! What happened to you?" A voice cut off Joe.

A bird sprinted toward the fallen bear.

"Woodie! Is it you?" Joe was surprised to see a familiar face.

"Yes it is me, I have a new home in the forest," said Woodie.

"You know him, Joe?" Becca inquired. Joe told Becca about Woodie, who had been his friend for over a year now.

"The bear needs urgent medical help. He isn't badly injured but if we don't get him free, he will die here", Woodie said with concern.

"There's a fox on the edge of the woods who is an herbalist. She can help us." Woodie continued.

They split into two teams; Woodie and Joe went on an expedition to find the fox. At the same time, Becca stayed with the injured bear. She remembered when she fell sick, and her mother cared for her. Her heart broke for the bear who lay there and had no one to look after him.

While the other team was headed to the herbalist, Joe could not contain his curiosity and asked Woodie how he found him in the woods. Woodie told Joe that every animal in the forest has its own superpowers, and nature has blessed Woodie with the superpower to hear voices from far away. He heard Joe yelling and came to rescue him when she discovered Rex was in trouble.

Madame Fox lived in the bushes at the edge of the forest. It was a long voyage but was worth it since Joe was enjoying the rescue operation in the forest. They reached the hut of the old herbalist who wore rounded glasses that resembled Harry Potter's. Woodie described the situation and requested her help.

"Well, you see, I am an old fox now. I haven't even eaten for three days because I can't go hunting. I am too weak to travel long distances," said Madame Fox in dismay.

"We can bring you some berries!" said Joe. "You can eat them and get the energy to come with us." Joe was happy to have solved the issue.

They wandered around and found a tree of berries. Joe stuffed his pockets with berries, and they returned to the fox den. After she had eaten all the berries, she felt healthy enough to go treat her patient.

They voyaged back to where they had left Rex and Becca.

"We're back," announced Joe.

Becca sighed; she was relieved to see Madame Fox with them. She had been sitting there with Rex, contemplating what would happen if they were unable to rescue the poor bear in pain. But they made it. They were back with a forest doctor!

Madame Fox took charge. She instructed Joe and Becca to pry the rocks while she pulled out Rex's paw. Then, she cut open some aloe vera, used the gel to disinfect the wound, and applied some herbs that would reduce the pain. She poured a tonic into Rex's mouth to nourish him with energy. In a flurry of moments, Rex opened his eyes and murmured, "Wa..wat-er." Becca rushed to pour water from her bottle into his mouth.

"How do you feel? sturdy fellow" asked Madame Fox after he had gulped in enough water.

"Fine," Rex smiled with gratitude.

"The job is done," said Madame Fox.

Tears burst out of Becca's and Joe's eyes, and they hugged each other joyfully. Woodie kept fluttering here and there in joy. While Rex expressed his gratitude to everyone involved, Madame Fox bandaged his wound. It really turned out to be a once-in-a-lifetime experience for Joe. He would surely spend the rest of his life reliving the moment when he helped save Rex's life.

WHISPERING PINES

The day was finally here, the annual 6th-grade camping trip. Lily and her friends had been looking forward to this trip all year. She had spent last night packing, and repacking, making sure she had the perfect outfits and didn't forget anything important.

The trip would only last three days, and Lily was certain that she over-packed. She was worried she would forget some essential items.

As the sun set behind the tall pine trees, Lily and her best friends Rose and Marie stepped off the yellow school bus and were greeted by the light breeze and the smell of nature. At the entrance of the camp, they had passed through an old wrought iron gate. Scrolled across the top of the gate were the words "Welcome to camp Whispering Pines". This would be their home for the weekend.

Although this camp was only an hour away from Lily's actual home, you would think they were halfway around the world. Rumors had been passed down from previous campers that this campground was haunted and in the middle of the night you could even hear strange, unexplained noises. But the students were not scared, to Lily and the rest of the 6th graders, this trip felt like a small taste of freedom.

It was a privilege and not everyone could attend this outing, you had to be on the honor roll all year to qualify, and that was not a simple accomplishment. One year of hard work earned you two nights of freedom, and it had been a hard year indeed. Lily had to stay after school every day for a week to do Math tutoring in order to stay on the honor roll.

As all the students gathered outside the bus, they were greeted by a few friendly faces in bright blue shirts with white block letters on the back that said "Staff". Everyone waited in line to be assigned to their cabins, all the girls in one cabin and all the boys in the other. The cabins were dark, dingy and pretty bare, just a wooden structure with a shared bathroom at the back. Each cabin had 10 sets of bunk beds, allowing 18 students and 2 chaperones just enough space to sleep.

Lily unpacked her sleeping bag and rolled it out on the mattress, placing her pillow on top. She zipped up her backpack and stuck it under her bed. She was assigned the bottom bunk, and although disappointed at first, she now appreciated the extra storage space she would have. The camp was buzzing with excitement as the students got ready for dinner in the dining hall, but the main event scheduled for the evening was the campfire.

Lily could hardly wait to be sitting around the warm fire, making s'mores and giggling with her friends. Dinner was nothing fancy, just some sloppy joes and Kraft mac and cheese. The meal was only slightly better than the lunch food they served at school. Everyone sat at long picnic-style tables in the dining hall, greedily eating their meal, it was clear they were all in a hurry to get out to the fire.

The students began to gather around the fire, finding seats on folding chairs, logs and large rocks that were placed close enough to feel the heat and for their roasting sticks to reach the flames. There was a table covered with marshmallows, graham crackers and Hershey's milk chocolate squares. One of the people in the blue shirt gave instructions on how to roast the marshmallow, black and crispy on the outside, and melty and sticky on the inside. That is the secret to the perfect ooey, gooey s'more. There were options to use peanut butter cups or white chocolate squares, but Lily loved a traditional milk chocolate s'more, it was a classic that didn't need to be improved.

The sun was beginning to set and everyone was on their second sweet treat by the time Jackson, a boy in Lily's class, spoke up and said his older brother was at this camp a few years ago and he had a story to tell. He began retelling a creepy tale about strange noises that could only be heard at night. He told about how his brother and his friends were kept up all night by the sounds but were never able to solve the mystery. He said his brother's dreams were still haunted to this day by the unknown source.

Lily and her friends were listening to the story about monsters in the woods in disbelief, rolling their eyes while Jackson tried his best to convince them he was telling the truth. To the girls, there was no way this was a true story. All of a sudden, the students heard a scream come from somewhere behind the boy, deep in the woods, along the trail that goes to the lake. The staff members looked at each other and smiled.

Slowly, Lily and her friends stood up, clutching each other but determined to be brave. They stepped towards the trail and looked ahead as it disappeared into the dark woods. Determined to uncover the source of the noises, they grabbed the only flashlight that was nearby and began moving towards the path that led to the lake. Lily caught the eye of a staff member who smiled and nodded, silently giving permission for the group to begin their quest as Jackson could be heard yelling "I told you so" and "I told you it was a true story".

The worn trail led through the dense woods, where more trees were casting twisted dark shadows that looked like hands reaching out to them as the dim light of the sunset gave way to the dark night. Tall tales of hauntings and ghosts ran through their minds. There was an air of excitement, unknown, and to be honest, fear as the girls crept along the trails lit now only by the single beam coming from the flashlight.

The friends traveled deeper into the forest. Each step caused a rustle of leaves that echoed through the forest as they listened for any sign of the strange scream, and whoever or whatever had caused it.

They passed by the old abandoned original campground that had been used before the cabins and dining hall had been built. This just elevated the mystery as they could see the dormant fire pits, where students once sat around telling eerily similar stories of things that go bump in the night. The smell of pine and smoke from the campfire mingled together in the air.

The trio jumped as they heard the sound again, but this time closer as they were moving further along the trail. At that exact moment, something moved above them - among the treetops. Were they being followed? Had whatever caused the scream found them? They shined the light in the treetops but saw nothing but darkness and branches. Marie wanted to turn back, but Lily and Rose forced her to continue.

Cautiously they walked along the path, holding hands so they didn't lose each other. Up ahead they could see the stars shining on the lake. They looked like fireflies dancing. Again, they heard the scream, this time directly above them. It sounded like a wounded cat, but how could a cat be in the tree?

Just as the girls were about to turn around and run back to the fire, something moved above their heads. Their lights caught the reflection of two eyes staring back at them. There really was something in the woods!

Rose screamed, Lily jumped and Marie dropped the flashlight, leaving only darkness in front of them. By now, Lily and her friends were standing at the edge of the lake, their pulses racing, their hearts pounding. The echoes of the scream were bouncing off the trees, to finally end, leaving them with the stillness of the night. They moved together searching for the source of the scream.

And then, as if on cue, Marie picked up the flashlight and shined it into the treetops. The full moon cast just enough light to illuminate the silhouette of a bird's nest and an owl perched high above them. The owl's eyes glowed back at them like orbs in the darkness. This is what they had seen staring back at them. The owl spread its wings and the girls took a step back, afraid she might attack.

As they stared in disbelief at how silly they were being, the owl opened his mouth and let out the most terrifying sound. It cut right through the silence. A sound that could easily be mistaken for a scream. Once again, it echoed through the trees, seeming to bounce back and forth around them, sending shivers down their spines.

It was at this time that the realization came to Lily and her friends. The scream that had sent them hunting down the source in the woods, the scream that had initiated the fear and bravery was nothing more than the haunting hoots of an owl piercing the tranquil night.

You could almost feel the relief wash over the group as their shoulders relaxed and they let their guards down. The fear that once had them frozen, was replaced by the wonder and awe of the wilderness. As the owl still sat perched among the trees high above them, the group turned to make their way back to the others at the campfire.

Excitement was buzzing, like electricity in the air, beneath the canopy of stars. Lily, Rose and Marie gathered around, keeping warm by the crackling campfire. Their faces were lit up by the warm glow and their minds racing from the adventure.

They were met by their fellow campers and a few staff members who looked at them knowingly as they recalled the story of their adventure. Lily was certain the staff knew what they would find, but was grateful to have been given the opportunity and freedom to explore.

The girls now realized, sometimes the mystery of the unknown can have a simple explanation. In the end, it was not monsters that lurked in the woods, just waiting for their next camper, as Jackson had believed. It was simply the beauty and wonder of nature, just waiting to be discovered. This was going to be an epic weekend!

The Unexpected Storm

Noah, a nine-year-old boy, was living the best of his life. He had his parents around, a big sister named Emma, and his grandparents, who were always there to shower him with love. He was exploring life and learning to understand the world.

But today, he was happy and excited for the first big adventure of his life. His mother was packing the items they might need on a one-night camping trip. She hustled all over the house; no one could just relax, because his mother was nervously double-checking and instructing everyone.

It was a happy occasion, but Noah could not understand why his mother was all stressed out. She had become a pendulum moving to and fro between the house and the stuffed-up car trunk. She didn't have a math test today; still, she seemed very nervous as if there was one.

She had checked the emergency kit dozens of times, confirmed that the tents were weather resistant, and made sure that his father would bring a multi-tool and repair kit including a knife, screwdriver, and duct tape.

Noah could not understand his mother. Why do adults make everything so complicated? He was stuck on this question when his father called him from the porch, and he rushed outside. The car was ready, and his father was there waiting for the family to get in the car. Noah hopped into the car and could not control his excitement. Noah could see trees beside the road and the sun synchronizing its movement with the car as they drove towards the campground.

On their way to their destination, they witnessed a diverse landscape that left Noah awestruck. The sun was casting its golden glow on the car as a warm welcome for the family while they drove on the winding roads. Noah, grinning from ear to ear with joy, peered out of the car window, his eyes wide open as he witnessed the lush greenery and the enchanting landscape.

His excitement for the adventure that lay ahead kept him wide-eyed. His older sister, Emma, was there, sitting beside him, her nose buried in a book. She occasionally took her eyes off the book to see her brother's excitement.

In the driver's seat sat his father, who was casually enjoying his day off from life and humming alongside the radio's tune. At the same time, his mother was busy gazing at her tablet, tapping and typing as if she were a research student, collecting data for her project. His mother was a meticulous planner and had a disposition for worrying. She was intensely researching the region, understanding the map, and looking into the weather forecast of the area.

If you took a peek inside the car, you would feel the bubble of tranquility. The car was a mobile capsule of family time and serenity. Noah, in addition to looking at the views, was dreaming of the campfire, the hikes, and the stories that he would share with his friends after the trip. His eyes sparkled as he thought of all the adventures waiting ahead. He loved this trip, an opportunity to explore the world and live a day away from his hectic and boring school life.

Noah and his family were inhaling the serenity when his mother's sharp gasp changed the mood. "Ohh No!!" she exclaimed, her eyes a reflection of shock and alarm. She locked her eyes on the tablet and exclaimed, "the campsite is expected to be hit by a heavy storm tonight." His father was as relaxed as he always was. He shared a glance with his wife and negated the danger with a calm smile, stating, "Honey, it's just a prediction. Weather forecasts keep changing all the time; do not stress over it."

Noah's mother did not buy the logic, and she continued swiping and tapping her tablet screen in haste. She was now planning something. While she was hovering over the screen, she suggested, "We need to book a hotel room in case of emergency. I am going through the options, and we can select one of these. We should not go there without a plan B."

Noah was petrified that the camping adventure might be derailed, and his heart sank. He turned to his father with his hopeful and pleading eyes. His father could sense

Noah's disappointment and spoke with reassurance, "Honey, we are only here overnight. Let's not panic and enjoy the day. The weather might hold up, and if not, we have our emergency supplies, so, relax."

But his mother wasn't convinced. Her maternal instinct kept warning her to keep her kids out of danger. She tried to calm herself and took a deep breath. She nodded as if trying to believe what her husband had just assured her. But her eyes still reflected a touch of worry. Again, she got busy on the tablet. Noah took a sigh of relief, and the car continued down the road, weaving between the forest trees. The trees on both sides of the road seemed to dance in the light breeze.

As they reached their destination, Noah looked up at the sky, clear and void of any clouds. The sun was casting playful shadows through the pattern of leaves. He was relieved that an unexpected storm would not interfere with his trip. His excitement flashed through his face, and even Emma seemed interested in the campsite. She had put down the book she was reading and was gazing at the beautiful scenery.

Noah's family stepped out of their car, breathing in the fresh air and looking at the wonders of nature as they stood amidst the forest. Noah's parents started setting up the camp while the kids helped to carry things for them. Noah's father was keeping them busy with his witty comebacks and jokes. The kids were laughing, living, and enjoying every moment. His mother had even forgotten the storm and was just enjoying the trip.

They had now settled in their camp, filling the air with laughter and chatter. Noah helped his sister roast marshmallows over the campfire while the parents shifted food and other stuff from the car. The sky was now turning dark, even though it was afternoon.

All of a sudden, there was a pause in the tranquility as they heard a rumble of thunder in the distance. The thunder was instantly followed by raindrops. In a matter of minutes, the sky was covered by dark clouds unleashing a continuous downpour. They had not fully realized the sudden change in the weather when Noah witnessed their belongings being scattered around the campsite. The wind was so fierce that it was pulling at the tent.

"Noah, grab the tent poles," his father shouted. Noah tried his best to help, but one of the poles had bent out of shape. "We need a screwdriver. Where is the repair kit?" asked Noah's father. Noah's mother pointed to the car while sprinting to ship the supplies into the tent to prevent them from soaking.

Noah ran to the car and grabbed the kit. While his father screwed the pole, he held the tent pole steady, fighting the wind. Now, his mother and sister were inside the tent with all their supplies. It took them a few moments to have the tent settled and fixated properly.

The rain was picking up with every moment, the heavens had opened up. The heavy rain started, and both of them rushed inside the tent. Noah's father zipped up the tent tightly. Noah was shivering with fear and cold when his mother offered him a dry and warm jacket with a hot cup of hot chocolate.

The frightening voices of clouds rumbling continued to intimidate the kids when Noah's mother took out the cards and suggested playing. While the clouds continued pouring down, the family was enjoying some fun time together, Noah laughing at his father's jokes. There, Noah realized that places don't matter as much as people do. He was enjoying the game while the world outside was in true chaos.

Eventually, the rain and wind had stopped. The storm had passed and had left a renewed and fresh world. Noah's father knew they needed a room in a hotel. It was too risky to stay at the campsite during the night because the storm could hit the site again. He was going through the hotels in proximity when Noah's mother revealed that she had already booked two rooms in the hotel.

She revealed that she had foreseen the situation and hence could not help but keep the plan B prepared for unsolicited events. Noah's father smiled and expressed his gratitude. He was relieved because he knew his family would be safe now.

Noah was proud of his mother's foresight and intelligence. His eyes sparkled with pride for his mother. As they piled into the car, Noah felt the joy of a storm survivor who had helped his father protect his family. He felt overjoyed by this adventure and had learned to stay prepared for the worst situations.

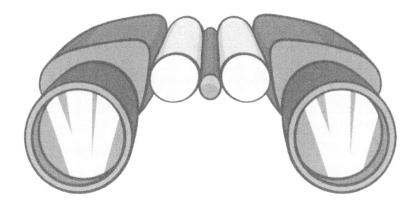

Title:_____

Title:_____

Title:_____

VI. TYPES OF FIRES AND SAFETY

Camping involves outdoor activities, and a key element is the campfire. Campfires are fires lit at campsites around a gathering spot. Campfires are not only one type; there are many. Each one is constructed based on what needs to be the final result. Let's understand some of the most common types of campfires.

- **Teepee fire** is a fire lit in a conical shape, which mimics a teepee. In this, the firewood is arranged in a cone shape to provide good airflow and efficient combustion.
- **Log cabin fire** is usually created with small and large firewood pieces. They are alternately stacked, forming a square or log cabin-esque structure.
- **Lean-to-fire** is the type in which a large log is horizontally arranged, with smaller firewood pieces leaned against it at an angle. It's effective in windy conditions because the large log is used as a windbreak.
- **Star fire** is arranged in a star, sometimes an asterisk-shape, focusing at the center. It's usually used as a favorite central gathering point. It is quite beneficial for cooking or hosting a group around the fire.
- **A Dakota fire hole** requires digging a hole and then is connected to a second hole by a tunnel. One hole is for the fire, and the other serves as a vent. This fire gives minimal smoke.
- **Reflector fire** needs a back wall erected right behind the main fire. It's done using rocks or logs to reflect heat to the campsite. It's highly effective in cold weather.

Minimizing the impact of campfire

While campfires are enjoyable, campers need to follow safety precautions for their well-being as well as for the environment. According to a report by Children's Hospital of Wisconsin, more than half of camping injuries in children are caused by campfire burns. So, without safety measures, large open flames can turn into a night in the emergency department. As we strive for safety, here are a few ways to actually achieve it.

1. Using only designated fire rings/pits
Usually, places that are known for camping have already established fire rings and pits. So always use them.

2. Keep fires small
Another thing you can do is to limit the size of your campfire as needed for essentials like cooking and roasting marshmallows. The smaller the fire, the less fuel it will require and, in return, will produce a lower environmental impact.

3. Use small, dead, and downed wood
Using already broken branches will avoid cutting down living trees and also clean up underbrush which can contribute to forest fires.

4. Be mindful of location
You need to choose a location for your fire, and it must be 200 feet away from lakes and streams, to protect the water

quality. Also, keeping a good distance from vegetation (forest) is recommended.

5. Respect fire bans

When you see fire ban signs and prohibitions regarding lighting a fire in any particular area, follow them. These signs are put on keeping in mind the dry conditions and knowing that open fires have a high risk of wildfires in that area.

6. Extinguish fires completely

When you are about to leave the site, make sure that the campfire is fully extinguished. You can pour some water on the fire and make sure the ashes get cool to touch. It can get dangerous to leave a fire unattended.

7. Pack out ashes

Part of practicing No Trace camping involves cleaning up your ashes. When you leave your site, wind or other factors can scatter the ashes of your fire making a mess. It's better to pack them in a container or put them in a garbage bin to keep the campsite looking clean, sustainable and ready for the next campers. Burying them is another great way to go.

VII. Coloring, Tic Tac Toe, Scavenger hunts, blank Treasure Maps, Word Search and Notes

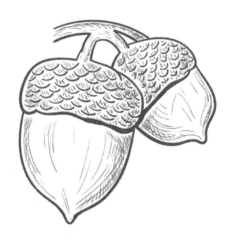

Draw | Doodle | Inspire

Draw | Doodle | Inspire

Draw | Doodle | Inspire

Draw | Doodle | Inspire

Draw | Doodle | Inspire

TIC TAC TOE

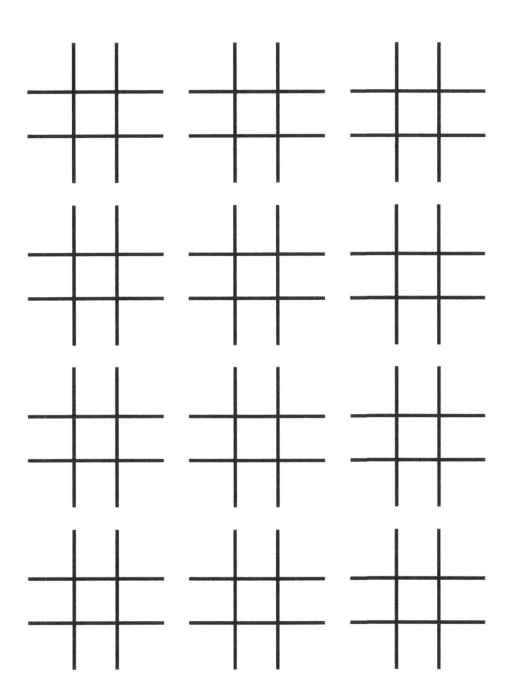

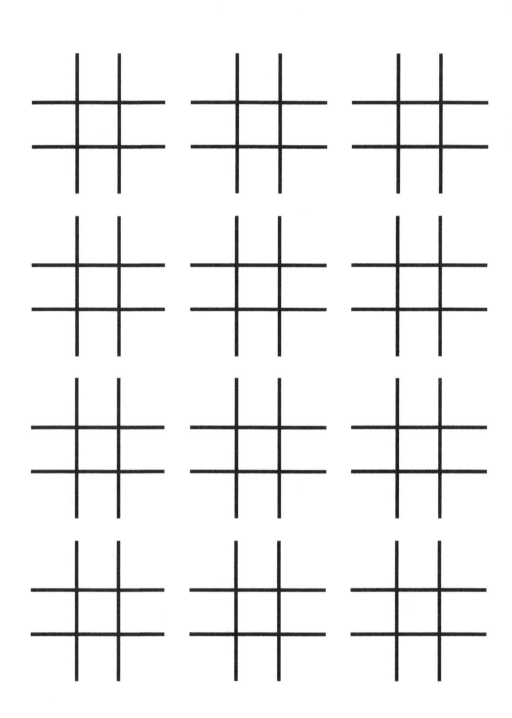

TIC TAC TOE

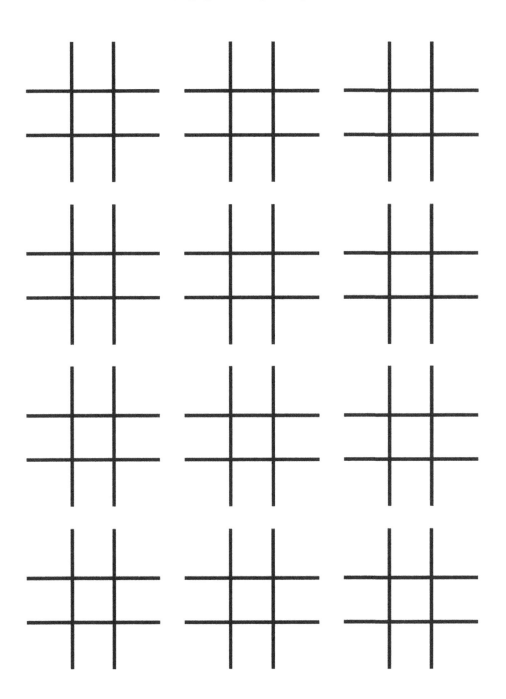

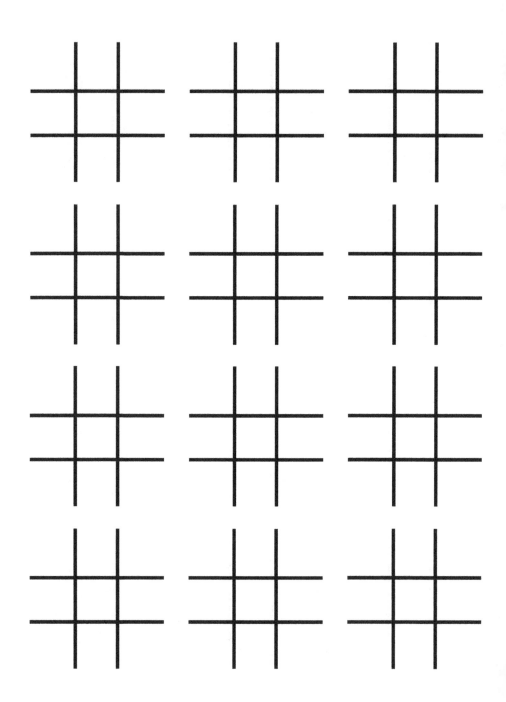

TIC TAC TOE

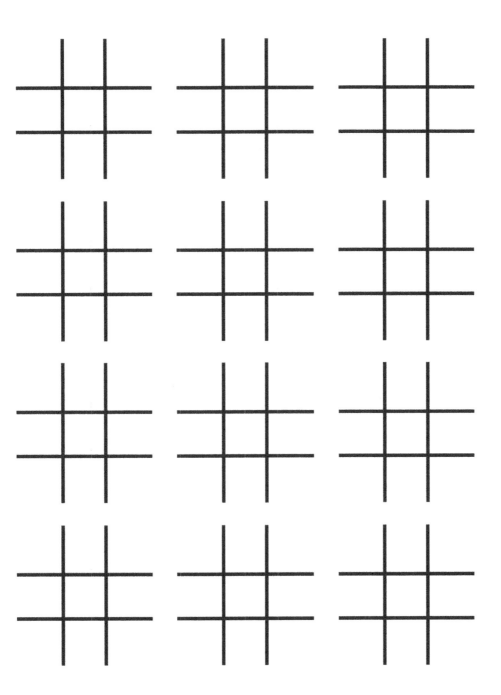

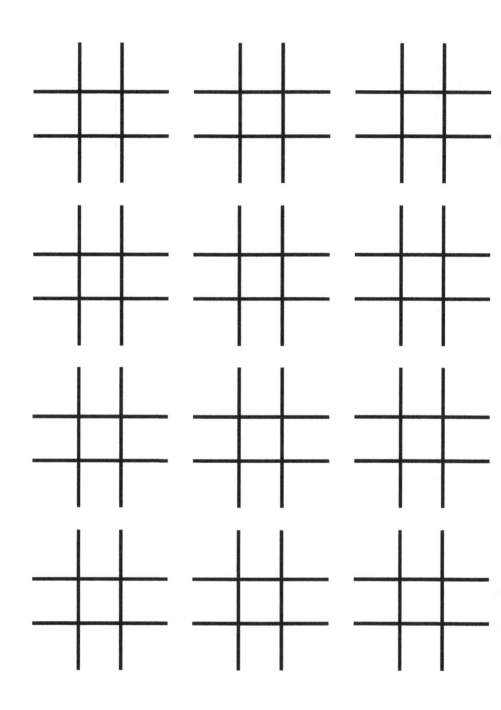

TIC TAC TOE

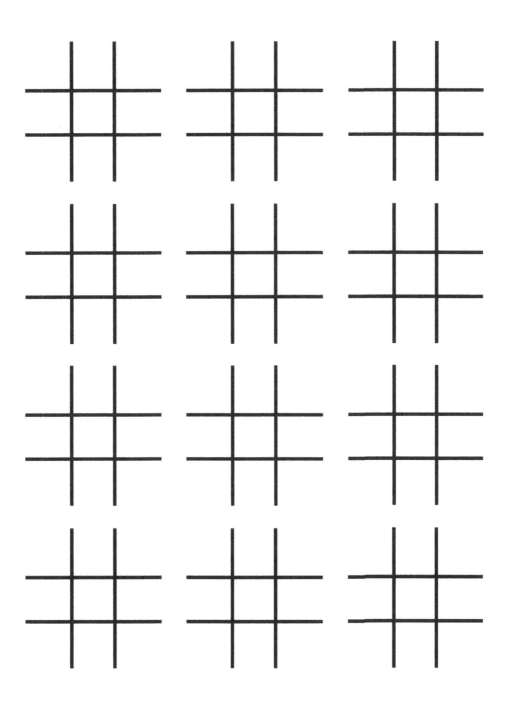

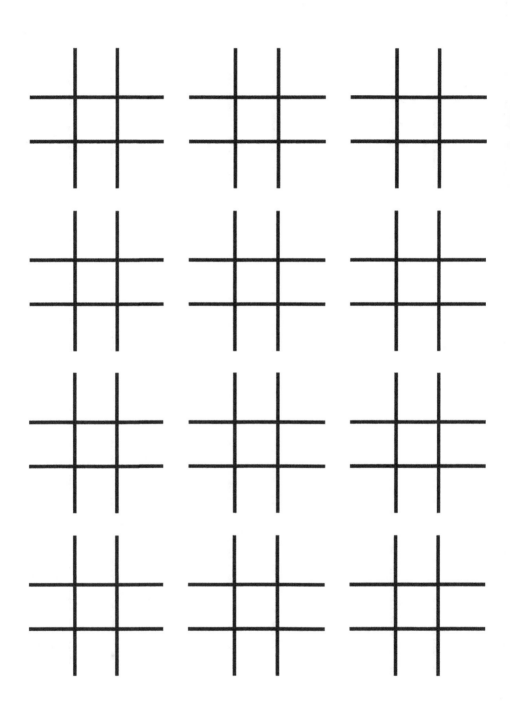

Scavenger hunt

- ☐ A Pine Cone
- ☐ A Spider's Web
- ☐ First Aid Kit
- ☐ A rock as big as your hand
- ☐ A Stick as long as your arm
- ☐ A Mushroom
- ☐ A Bird's nest
- ☐ A deck of cards
- ☐ A Tarp
- ☐ A Flashlight
- ☐ An insect
- ☐ A Backpack
- ☐ The Moon
- ☐ The Sun
- ☐ A Sleeping Bag
- ☐ A Star in the Sky
- ☐ A campfire
- ☐ A Map
- ☐ Firewood
- ☐ A Flower

Scavenger hunt

- [ ] _____
- [ ] _____
- [ ] _____
- [ ] _____
- [ ] _____
- [ ] _____
- [ ] _____
- [ ] _____
- [ ] _____
- [ ] _____
- [ ] _____
- [ ] _____
- [ ] _____
- [ ] _____
- [ ] _____
- [ ] _____
- [ ] _____
- [ ] _____

TREASURE HUNT MAP

TREASURE HUNT MAP

N E S W

TREASURE HUNT MAP

CAMPING WORD SEARCH

```
C O M P A S S E O Z F T B
A S O O W L G B P R I P I
M Q A Q R E H P M F R S N
P U M R I E O O P W E P O
F I A O O P S F T P W L C
I R U P U I T I C D O O U
R R A E R N S H A E O S L
E E M K E G T M M X D G A
I L H T W B O A P A E P R
F I I B E A R P I Z V R S
H I K I N G Y S N N A I M
O F L A S H L I G H T S P
B A C K P A C K H W W W W
```

CAMPING   AXE   BACKPACK   BEAR   BINOCULARS   CAMPFIRE

COMPASS   FIREWOOD   FLASHLIGHT   GHOSTSTORY   HIKING   HOTDOG

MOUNTAIN   OWL   ROPE   SLEEPINGBAG   SQUIRREL   TENT

NOTES

NOTES

NOTES

CAMPING WORD SEARCH - ANSWERS
SHEET

CAMPING AXE BACKPACK BEAR BINOCULARS CAMPFIRE

COMPASS FIREWOOD FLASHLIGHT GHOSTSTORY HIKING HOTDOG

MOUNTAIN OWL ROPE SLEEPINGBAG SQUIRREL TENT

SCAN ME

IF YOU ENJOYED
THIS BOOK, PLEASE
LEAVE A REVIEW.
YOUR KIND WORDS AND
REVIEWS ARE GREATLY
APPRECIATED!

Made in the USA
Las Vegas, NV
12 July 2024

92226152R00066